Barrelhouse and Boogi

by Eric Kriss

Order No. OK 64659
International Standard Book Number: 0.8256.0059.6
Library of Congress Catalog Card Number: 72-97852

Exclusive Distributors:
Music Sales Corporation
257 Park Avenue South, New York, NY 10010 U.S.A.
Music Sales Limited
8/9 Frith Street, London W1V 5TZ England
Music Sales Pty. Limited
120 Rothschild Street, Rosebery, Sydney, NSW 2018, Australia

Printed in the United States of America by
Vicks Lithograph & Printing Corporation

Oak Publications
London/New York/Sydney/Cologne

Recording Excerpts and Credits

Jelly Roll Blues/Jelly Roll Morton. Used by permission of Biograph Records.*
Dyin' Rider Blues/Romeo Nelson. Used by permission of Folkways Records.
Mercy Blues/Barrelhouse Buck. Used by permission of Folkways Records.
Dying Pickpocket Blues/Barrelhouse Welsh. Issued on Yazoo 1028.**
State Street Jive/Cow Cow Davenport. Issued on Yazoo 1028.**
I Don't Know/Cripple Clarence Lofton. Issued on Yazoo 1025.**
Peetie Wheatstraw Stomp/William Bunch (Wheatstraw). From Arhoolie LP BC4.***
Indiana Avenue Stomp/Montana Taylor. Issued on Yazoo 1028.**
Fat Fanny Stomp/Jim Clark.
Big Fat Mama/Walter Roland. Issued on Yazoo 1017.**
Honky Tonk Train/Meade Lux Lewis. Used by permission of Folkways Records.
I Need a Little Spirit/Dave Alexander. From Arhoolie LP 1067.***
Sail On Blues/Memphis Slim. Used by permission of Folkways Records.
Whistlin' Alex Moore's Blues/Alex Moore. From Arhoolie LP 1008.***
The Cows/Robert Shaw. From Arhoolie LP B1010.***
Sugarland Blues/Black Boy Shine. From Arhoolie LP BC7.***
Atlanta Bounce/Piano Red. From Arhoolie LP 1064.***
It's You Baby/Sunnyland Slim. Used by permission of Storyville Records.
I Can Tell by the Way You Smell/Walter Davis. Issued on Yazoo 1025.**
Lonesome Day Blues/Jesse James.
Short Haired Blues/Kid Stormy Weather. From Arhoolie LP BC7.***
Stella Blues/Oliver (Dink) Johnson. Used by permission of William Russell.

* From *Jelly Roll Morton, Blues and Stomps* (piano rolls). BLP 1004 Q, Biograph Records Inc., Box 109, Canaan, N.Y. 12029.
** These recordings can be heard in their entirety on their respective Yazoo LP's. A free catalog is available by writing to Yazoo Records, 245 Wavery Place, New York, N.Y. 10014. Yazoo records may be ordered by mail from Yazoo.
*** For their complete catalog of over 150 Blues and Folk LP's and a free copy of the *Arhoolie Occasional*, send fifty cents to: Chris Strachwitz, Arhoolie Records, Box 9195, Berkeley, Ca. 94709.

PHOTOGRAPHS
Ramsey Archive: Pages 9, 23, 30, and 112 (Meade Lux Lewis)
Courtesy of Arhoolie Records/By Chris Strachwitz: Pages 68 and 112 (Alex Moore and Piano Red)
Courtesy of Living Blues: Page 16
Courtesy of Jim O'Neal: Pages 6 and 80
By Eric Kriss: Pages 36, 85, 94, and 112 (Dave Alexander)
By Sandy Sutherland/Courtesy Jim O'Neal: Pages 112 (Boogie Woogie Red)
Courtesy of Eric Kriss and Romeo Nelson: Page 19

Book design by Jean Hammons

Contents

Acknowledgments 4
Introduction 5

Ragtime Blues 7
Jelly Roll Blues/*Jelly Roll Morton* 10
Barrelhouse and Boogie 13
Dyin' Rider Blues/*Romeo Nelson* 17
Mercy Blues/*Barrelhouse Buck* 20
Dying Pickpocket Blues/*Barrelhouse Welch* 22
State Street Jive/*Cow Cow Davenport* 24
I Don't Know/*Cripple Clarence Lofton* 26
Stomps and Struts 31
Peetie Wheatstraw Stomp/*Peetie Wheatstraw* 34
Indiana Avenue Stomp/*Montana Taylor* 37
Fat Fanny Stomp/*Jim Clarke* 42
Big Fat Mama/*Walter Roland* 45
Boogie Woogie 48
Honky Tonk Train/*Meade Lux Lewis* 53
Sail On Blues/*Memphis Slim* 56
I Need a Little Spirit/*Dave Alexander* 58
Whistlin' Alex Moore's Blues/*Alex Moore* 61
Roll and Tumble 65
The Cows/*Robert Shaw* 69
Sugarland Blues/*Black Boy Shine* 73
Atlanta Bounce/*Piano Red* 76
It's You Baby/*Sunnyland Slim* 78
Barrelhouse Blues 81
Lonesome Day Blues/*Jesse James* 83
I Can Tell By the Way You Smell/*Walter Davis* 86
Stella Blues/*Dink Johnson* 88
Short Haired Blues/*Kid Stormy Weather* 90

Exercises 95
Coordination 95
Fingering 97
Tremelo 98
Further Reading 99
Discography 100
Part I - Barrelhouse and Boogie 100
Part II - Suggested Piano Blues Albums 104
Appendix A-Barrelhouse and Boogie Bass Lines 105
Appendix B-Record Company Addresses 111

Acknowledgements

Many people have assisted me in my exploration of blues piano. Without the encouragement, understanding and editorial abilities of my wife, Barbara, I would have been lost in a pile of music paper and notes. Jim O'Neal provided valuable photographs and historical material from the Living Blues archives and showed me around the back alleys of Chicago. I am grateful to Dave Alexander, Sunnyland Slim, Little Brother Montgomery, Jimmy Walker and Erwin Helfer for sharing their personal views about their lives as musicians and about the music they play. I would also like to thank Larry Leitch, who helped transcribe five recordings, Chris Strachwitz of Arhoolie Records, and Paul Garon.

–Eric Kriss

Introduction

Before the juke box, radio and television, the wandering musician provided much of America's entertainment. He spread the news, the fashions and the jokes. An aura of mystery surrounded him. In black communities, this tradition was especially powerful and every Saturday night folks crowded into honky tonks, bars and barrelhouses to hear a new sound. This was the world of the blues piano player: sitting in a corner all night, pounding out stomps, low-down blues, fast boogies, drinking beer, shouting and having a whopping good time. It was a fast scene and the life expectancy wasn't too long, but thousands of men chose to leave family and job behind to follow the rough lumber camps, haunt roadside barrelhouses or drift through dusty, obscure hamlets in search of an audience. This book is about the music these musicians created.

In the hundred years since the birth of piano blues, many styles have come and gone, with only a few permanently etched on record. Some piano players like Roosevelt Sykes and Memphis Slim have received well-deserved recognition, but most of the wandering blues pianists have vanished, leaving behind only a scratchy 78 or two and their colorful names: Kid Stormy Weather, Black Boy Shine, Barrelhouse Welch, Drive 'Em Down, Toothpick, Big Jug, No Leg Kenny, Trigger Sam, Game Kid, Burnt Face; the list goes on.

The twenty-two pianists I have chosen represent a broad spectrum, from the bawdy entertainer to the introspective soloist. The pieces were selected for originality, virtuosity and availability; it seemed senseless to discuss music that was never recorded or a musician whose records remain unissued. I have also excluded the pianists described in my first book, *Six Blues-Roots Pianists*. These influential musicians deserve careful study: Jimmy Yancey, Champion Jack Dupree, Little Brother Montgomery, Speckled Red, Roosevelt Sykes and Otis Spann. I suggest that *Six Blues-Roots Pianists* be used as a companion book with this one.

Barrelhouse and Boogie Piano contains several valuable learning aids: the 12-minute recording of selected piano blues excerpts; the Appendix of barrelhouse and boogie piano bass lines; a section of exercises; and a piano blues discography and bibliography.

The enclosed recording is especially useful as an introduction to blues piano styles–the phrasing, syncopation and intensity of the music can really be understood only after repeated listening. The complete recordings, however, should be consulted whenever possible, for the short excerpts do have limited scope. The discography has a complete list of all the recordings mentioned in the text (as well as other suggested recordings) and the appendix of record companies addresses should facilitate the task of locating these elusive releases.

The exercises concentrate on many of the unique problems of blues piano: the coordination of the right hand with a boogie bass; the fingering of blues grace notes and runs; and the rough touch but steady control of barrelhouse style. The appendix of bass lines, aside from being a reference guide to blues piano styles, provides a point of departure for extending melodic phrases into complete blues compositions.

Finally a word about the twenty-two transcriptions. Every attempt has been made to faithfully duplicate the original music on record within the limited boundaries of musical notation. Some of the rhythms and phrases are so idiosyncratic that a precise transcription would be hopelessly complicated. Accordingly, I have tried to find the right balance between accuracy and practicality. The transcriptions are intended only as guides to playing piano blues and the original recordings must be religiously consulted to master the nuances and complexities of this rich piano tradition.

Roosevelt Sykes, a master of the barrelhouse blues.

Ragtime Blues

New Orleans was the stomping grounds for all
the greatest pianists in the country.

—Jelly Roll Morton

Jelly Roll Morton played a blend of blues, ragtime jazz and classical music which I call *ragtime blues.* Although many pianists once performed in this style, few examples have been preserved. Morton was a Creole, a word that is almost synonymous with new Orleans jazz, and he developed his music under unique social circumstances which merged Creole culture with the blues roots of Louisiana blacks.

The evolution of the word *creole* tells us something about the environment that made ragtime blues possible. According to the 1604 edition of D'Acosta's *History of the West Indies,* the word *crollos* was first used to distinguish between Spaniards born in the West Indies and those born in Spain. When the French inhabitants of the Louisiana Territory adopted the word, they modified the pronunciation to *creole* and applied it to themselves and many of their possessions. Thus, French children in Louisiana were called Creoles, French cuisine became Creole cooking, and the African slaves of the Frenchmen were Creole slaves. In everyday usage, the slaves took to calling themselves Creoles too, although they often added the phrase *of Color* to distinguish their status from the white Creoles. By the 18th century, the term *Creole of Color* meant a mulatto born on American soil whose position was inferior to the whites but superior to the blacks.

The Creoles of Color, or simply Creoles as they came to be known when most whites ceased to use the term, lived in an uneasy world defined by the Black Code of 1724. This Code gave freedom to all children of racially mixed unions upon the death of the white partner, who was almost invariably the father. Until his death, the mulatto children shared the slave status of their black mother.

The situation was certainly ambiguous. How could a mulatto slave, who would be freed upon the death of his white father, be expected to live as a free man without an education and proper upbringing? On the other hand, how could an educated mulatto still be a slave? Wealthy households, recognizing the need to prepare the Creoles for a free life, provided an education at French schools and offered many of the advantages of the white world. But Creoles were not regarded as equals by the white society, so they established their own "aristocracy" modeled after the whites; in fact, by the mid-1800's, many Creoles of New Orleans had amassed considerable personal fortunes.

In 1894 everything began to change. After one hundred and fifty years of living like whites, the Creoles were gradually forced out of profitable jobs by a new code which forbade any special privileges and relegated the Creoles to the position of their blacker neighbors. This change in Creole status had a profound influence upon the birth of ragtime in the mid-1890's.

Jelly Roll Morton was born in 1885 to a respectable Creole family. In Alan Lomax's *Mister Jelly Roll,* Morton describes his ancestors as Frenchmen, and the relatives he knew were "never able to speak a word in American or English." His grandfather, a wholesaler of "fine liquors" named Julien Monette, was elected state senator and served in the Louisiana Constitutional Convention of 1868, but by the time Morton was 10 years old, that world of power and wealth was closed to a Creole forever. Being an ambitious young man, he turned instead to a world that would accept him, the red-light district of Storyville, where he earned a living as a pool shark, gambler, piano player and teller of wild tales.

Morton was exposed to both European instruments and primitive music makers like the jew's harp, tin pan drum and box guitar. At the age of six he took guitar lessons from a "Spanish gentleman in the neighborhood" and, by his own description, became quite accomplished. Concerts at the French opera house inspired him to play the piano but he didn't take it up because "the piano was known in our circle as an instrument for a lady."* A few years later, when Morton saw a gentleman play a manly ragtime, he changed his mind.

Morton studied the piano at St. Joseph's University, a Catholic college that believed in a rigorous approach, and it's not surprising that Morton's pieces frequently imitate classical forms like the rondo. He often wrote out every note of his arrangements, insisting that they be played exactly as notated. Like Scott Joplin and James P. Johnson, who considered themselves serious ragtime composers, Morton adamantly demanded discipline and the perfection of classical technique. So, when Creole musicians like Morton, with classical backgrounds, ventured into the red-light districts where blues was an established tradition, the music that came out was a blend of ragtime jazz, classical technique and earthy blues.

New Orleans in the 1890's was an exotic cosmopolitan center. Trade boomed along the Mississippi River and an endless promenade of African voodoo men, West Indian merchants, stylish aristocrats and Creoles lined the narrow streets of the French quarter. The Storyville section, known as The District, held an unrivaled position as a wide-open town in those days. The spread of bawdy houses, liquor, drugs, prostitution and gambling scandalized "respectable" society. One report quoted in Stephen Longstreet's *Sportin' House* described a dance as follows:

> *A hall would be filled with some two or three hundred scowling, black-bearded, red-shirted visitors coming from every port, prison and lazar-house, and presenting such a motley throng as Lafitte or any of the pirates of the Gulf might have gathered for their crews. With a piano . . . and with dances so abandoned and reckless . . . one can form an idea of what the scene was.*

It was here that Jelly Roll learned to play the blues from pianists like the three-fingered Mamie Desdoumes and the great Tony Jackson. *Jelly Roll Blues* was written during this period, in 1905, and was one of the first blues songs to be copyrighted (Morton, unlike many rural barrelhouse bluesmen, was quite a savvy businessman). Many recorded versions of the piece exist; the one transcribed here was taken from a piano roll made by Morton in 1924 and is currently available on Biograph BLP-1004Q.

Jelly Roll Blues is divided into five major themes (the first three themes are transcribed here) grouped in two movements as follows:

Introduction A A B B C C / Introduction D D E E E

*From Alan Lomax's *Mister Jelly Roll*, Grosset & Dunlap, 1950, p. 6.

Each section is based on a 12 bar progression, yet the progression is not strictly a blues one (that is, I / I / I / I / IV / IV / I / I / V / IV / I / I); rather, it is a synthesis of earlier ragtime numbers and blues. Joplin often used a 16 bar form totally unrelated to the standard blues progression, and his themes carried few blues riffs. Morton, on the other hand, explored the use of blues melodies and successfully incorporated rougher barrelhouse piano music into the tight structure of ragtime.

Play *Jelly Roll Blues* with precision, balanced with some good-time foot-banging. The glissando bass figure should be performed with a twist of the wrist, grouping the fingers closely together. All dotted eighths are given a weighted emphasis, like a march, but the piece should never become overbearing or stodgy.

Jelly Roll Blues/*Jelly Roll Morton*

by Jelly Roll Morton

tr

3
3
3
3
3
1.
tr
2.
8va
3
3
3
3
3
3
rit.

Barrelhouse and Boogie

What I mean by barrelhousing: barrelhousing it mean store-porching, and store-porching it mean one man be playin' a piano.

—Otis Spann

Barrelhouse

The tradition of barrelhouses, joints that featured a piano player banging out music until the wee hours of the morning, goes back a long time and figures prominently in the lives and legends of countless bluesmen. Leadbelly killed a man at a barrelhouse, Leroy Carr died dancing in one, and mysterious piano players like Kid Stormy Weather, Black Boy Shine and Barrelhouse Welch spent much of their lives in these hard-rocking, dimly-lit shacks. This violent atmosphere, totally segregated from the white world, bred a new kind of music, a piano style commonly called *barrelhouse.*

The original barrelhouses, modest wood structures with dirt floors (some had wooden planks for dancing), are rapidly vanishing from the American landscape, victims of floods, highway construction and, most of all, time. But even today, a few grace lonely backcountry roads, with Royal Crown Cola signs and hand-painted lettering proclaiming their names: "Lee and Bill's Vee-Country Inn," "Lazy D Rock 'n Roll Cafe," and "Hi-Time Cut-Rate Liquor, Beer & Gas." Modern conveniences have wrought changes. Many tavern owners installed juke boxes when electricity became available, to complement or replace the pianos; these places were labeled *juke joints,* although I've never seen the term actually used in the name of one.

The musical instruments in these establishments were not of the best quality. Constant changes in humidity (especially in the South where most juke joints and barrelhouses are not air-conditioned), weekend beer baths and cigarette burns quickly reduced once dignified pianofortes to a condition of perpetual disrepair. Musicians adapted to these circumstances with remarkable ingenuity, using the out of tune strings to approximate the sound of guitar blues by "spacing" the 12-tone scale until it corresponded more closely with blues tonality.

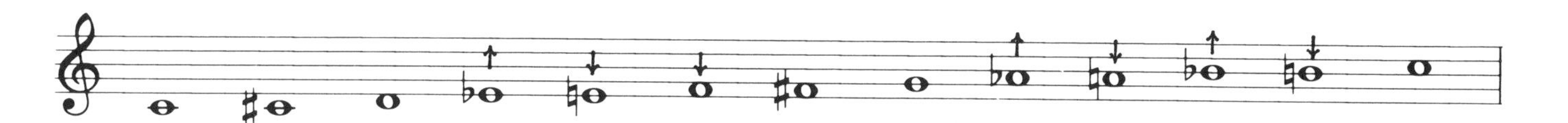

The "spacing" of the 12-tone scale

Many blues pianists still prefer to play old honky tonk uprights rather than risk the exacting performance of a concert grand.

Barrelhouse piano, which may have developed as early as 1870, was played by men who had no formal training on the instrument and therefore little or no familiarity with ragtime and its stylistic complexities. Most were self-taught or took a few "lessons" from respected players in their locality. Little Brother Montgomery, for example, learned barrelhouse riffs from Cooney Vaughn of Hattiesburg, Mississippi, and passed on his ideas to Lee Porkchops Green, who, in turn, showed them to Roosevelt Sykes. Champion Jack Dupree learned much of his early barrelhouse repertoire from Drive 'Em Down, a back-alley pianist from New Orleans. This informal transmission of music material made barrelhouse piano playing highly idiosyncratic, while the isolation of these musicians in backcountry joints reinforced a tradition of individuality. Thus Speckled Red, the composer of *The Dirty Dozens,* played 13 and 15 bar progressions (instead of the usual twelve), and the two-step blues of Barrelhouse Buck is not readily traceable to other barrelhouse forms.

Although compositions vary greatly from performer to performer, there are several striking characteristics of early barrelhouse piano playing. Structurally, the pieces tend to be simple song forms like A A A A or A A B A. Soloing is held to a minimum, frequently little more than right hand embellishments between vocal lines. Even these riffs are rarely improvized; mostly they are memorized and played over and over again with only insignificant variations. Harmonic arrangements stress a minor, hollow sound that uses open fifths and octaves to outline chord progressions. The chord progressions themselves lack much harmonic color, relying for the most part on simple triads and occasional 6ths and 7ths. There is also a notable absence of the dotted eighth note syncopations which later characterized so much of boogie piano music. Drone basses and simple alternating figures provide harmonic foundations for the right hand, but little rhythmic support.

Romeo Nelson, who lives today in a run-down tenement on Chicago's South Side, once toured successfully on the barrelhouse and honky tonk circuit. His *Gettin' Dirty Just Shakin' That Thing,* recorded in 1929, was a hit in the blues field and many older musicians remember him for his plaintive, primitive style. *Dyin' Rider Blues* is similar to one-chord guitar pieces, with a constant drone bass that dominates the harmony (see also *Highway 61 Blues* by Roosevelt Sykes in *Six Blues-Roots Pianists,* Oak Publications, 1973.) The empty, hollow sound is intentional and is emphasized by the rhythmic interplay between the piano accompaniment (in triplets) and the vocal line (in eighth notes).

Play the short bass glissando with a slight twist of the wrist, ending with the left thumb on E♭ . In classical piano technique, the thumb usually does *not* play the black notes in a run, but blues piano lends itself to a less delicate approach. Similarly, most chromatic passages should be played with a "sliding" finger motion. For example, the opening phrase is played with the first and third fingers; the third finger slides back and forth between G and G♭ .

"Sliding" finger motion

Dyin' Rider, originally recorded for Vocalion in 1929, has been reissued on RBF 12.

Thomas "Barrelhouse Buck" McFarland, born in Alton, Illinois in 1903, started playing for bawdy house parties at an early age. His two-step *Mercy Blues,* perhaps related to Cajun two-steps of Louisiana, centers around the syncopated turn in the bass line. The piece is based on a 12 bar blues progression with several personal idiosyncracies thrown in. The dominant chord (E♭ in this case), usually played in the 9th measure, makes a delayed appearance in the 10th and 11th bars while the 3rd chorus has a measure of $\frac{3}{4}$ added. This bouncy example of barrelhouse playing can be heard on Folkways 3554.

Not much is known about Barrelhouse Welch. In 1926 he made two brief appearances at the OKeh recording studio in Chicago, where he sang blues accompanied by Louis Armstrong, Richard M. Jones, the pianist, and Clarence Black, a studio violinist for OKeh. These recordings, four sides in all, were issued under the name Nolan Welsh. In 1929 he recorded for Paramount as Barrelhouse Welch, but only made two known sides, *Larceny Woman Blues* and *Dying Pickpocket Blues.*

Dying Pickpocket is a more sophisticated barrelhouse piece than *Mercy Blues* or *Dyin' Rider.* The left hand is a combination of an alternating and a walking bass line and the melody is filled with trills and blues grace notes. Pieces like *Dying Pickpocket* are transitional examples of the barrelhouse style as it developed from primitive and simple songs to the complex solos of pianists like Roosevelt Sykes. The original recording has been reissued on Yazoo 1028.

Boogie

As rural blacks migrated to urban centers, the old barrelhouses were replaced by rent house parties, a fascinating institution which arose in response to high rents. By charging admission to parties given in his apartment, a tenant was able to raise enough to keep a roof over his head. It wasn't long before these rent house parties acquired an air of professionalism: famous piano players were retained in advance, street corner advertisements lured potential customers and the real hot spots earned a respected notoriety throughout the neighborhood. The piano playing in the urban scene changed slightly, too—the barrelhouse style slowly became *boogie.*

Boogie piano, as distinguished from barrelhouse, relies on a strong, percussive bass line of continuously repeating riffs. The early examples (circa 1920 to 1927) retained most of the barrelhouse song forms and vocal material. But the powerful basses, perhaps a response to the noises of industrial society, gave boogie a different rhythmic feel, an exaggerated syncopation mixed with delicate polyrhythms.

Charles Davenport, the son of a Baptist minister, was an influential wandering bluesman who spread his barrelhouse/boogie style through Chicago's South Side, Detroit, and Cleveland. Born in 1894, Davenport failed to follow the religious course set out for him by his father, and traveled instead from one barrelhouse to the next as an entertainer. Although he recorded in 1925, Davenport's first big his was *Cow Cow Blues,* cut in 1928, which earned him the sobriquet Cow Cow Davenport.

State Street Jive, the flip-side of *Cow Cow Blues,* is a good example of hybrid barrelhouse/boogie compositions. The loose syncopated beat is in the boogie style, yet the limited soloing and repetitious song form is reminiscent of barrelhouse numbers. As with other "jive" pieces, the endless stream of chatter in *State Street* (about having a whopping good time and so forth) sets the mood for hard boogie dancing. The 1928 original has been reissued on Yazoo 1028.

Clarence Lofton, born a cripple, followed the same house party circuit as Cow Cow Davenport. Lofton incorporated many of Davenport's themes (*Cow Cow Blues* was one of his favorites) and added a fuller bass line, usually of doubled-up chromatic octaves. *I Don't Know,* recorded at a private session in the 1920's, illustrated Lofton's blend of boogie basses in a barrelhouse song format. Like Davenport, Lofton excelled as an entertainer whose playing reflected the evolution from barrelhouse to boogie blues. *I Don't Know* can be heard on Yazoo 1025 and has also been released on the Australian label, Swaggie 1235.

CHAMPION JACK DUPREE (Blues Singer with Inst. Acc.)

05823 Angola Blues
05713 Black Woman Swing
05713 Cabbage Greens No. 1
05823 Cabbage Greens No. 2

Before moving overseas, Champion Jack Dupree was active in the Indianapolis area where Montana Taylor played.

Dyin' Rider Blues/*Romeo Nelson*

by Romeo Nelson

let-ter from my rid-er
what do you reck-on it reads?
Hur-ry
home pa-pa rid-er's al-most dead.
1.2.
And I
D. S.
3.
go.

And I walked over, your dying rider say
And I walked over, your dying rider say
"Keep out of work," dying rider say.

Hurry home, dear papa, like you done before
Hurry home, dear papa, like you done before
I got a message from the angel, I guess I have to go.

Romeo Nelson

Mercy Blues/*Barrelhouse Buck*

3rd Chorus
1.
2.

Dying Pickpocket Blues/*Barrelhouse Welch*

by Barrelhouse Welch

And his buddy stood beside him with his long, dark silvered hair
And his buddy stood beside him with his long, dark silvered hair
Listenin' to the last words that the dyin' pickpocket say.

"Oh, so long partner, goin' to a better land
Oh . . . partner, goin' to a better land
I gone pick no more pockets, I'm goin' to be a regular man."

Although she has been a real pal and she answer to all my calls
Although she has been a real pal and she answer to all my calls
Yeah, ruin her health trying to spring me from this fall.

State Street Jive/*Cow Cow Davenport*

Cow Cow Davenport

State Street Jive/*Cow Cow Davenport*

by Charles "Cow Cow" Davenport

8va
rit.

I Don't Know/*Cripple Clarence Lofton*

by Cripple Clarence Lofton

Fast

Gon-na sit a-round for a while, should-a just rid-den
down this aisle. Dea-con Jones keep-in' a - pray - in',
got as much re - li - gion as one I've had. Wan-na go to heav-en got-ta
stop this stuff, Going to be strut - tin' that thing which - a - way?

I don't know, I don't know,
I don't know. I tell you
they're strut - tin' that thing night and
day.
1. D. S. 2.
1. D. S. 2.

8va
Solo
8va
8va
gliss.
gliss.
gliss.
8va
dim.

Shake it and break it, girls, you can hang it on the wall
Pitch it out the window, catch it before it fall
Stop a while, shimmy if it's all night long
Some time the thing's got your habit's on.

[Spoken] *But you shouldn't-a. Shouldn't-a what?*

Chorus:
I don't know, I don't know, I don't know,
I don't know.
I'm tellin you, honey, they're struttin' that thing
night and day.

Cripple Clarence Lofton

Stomps and Struts

Come on in now and get in this hip shaking contest.
Yeah, 'cause it's gonna be tight. Let's all of us
pull off our shoes and have a stinking good time.

—Hokum Boys, 1930

Thomas Edison, the man who started it all, had little idea what the record industry would become when he tinkered around with wax cylinders and made the first phonographs in 1877. At first people laughed, the customary response to new technological advances in those days, and paid to hear their own voices played back to them. In the 1880's, the idea of recording music for the general public caught on and by 1900 two firms, the Columbia Phonograph Company and Edison's National Phonograph Company, were selling cylinders everywhere. The introduction of the flat disc (the old cylinders were shaped like small cans) revolutionized the marketing of records and catapulted the industry to the forefront of the entertainment business.

In spite of the overwhelming public acclaim for the new inventions, record companies took about twenty-five years to realize the potential of ethnic markets like blues, jazz and bluegrass music. When the industry finally began to aggressively search out new talents on field trips and in regional studios, one of the most popular forms for the so-called race record market was the stomp—the hard-kicking, hip-shaking, fanny-twisting music that was part of every Saturday night barrelhouse party.

In many folk traditions, dance and music are inseparable cultural expressions. Unfortunately, the dance forms have been ignored by many music researchers and, accordingly, a vast amount of material has gone undocumented. (One of the few exceptions is *Jazz Dance*, a scholarly work by Marshall and Jean Stearns.) Only recently, in fact, have methods for describing dance in symbolic terminology been developed.

During the ragtime era, the *cakewalk*, a majestic striding step, caught the fancy of millions. A few photographic examples have been preserved as well as a remarkable sequence from a 1903 Edison film, *Uncle Tom's Cabin*, showing the "slaves" moving in a high-stepping cakewalk fashion. The dances for barrelhouse stomps were generally called *struts*, but the term broadly applies to hundreds of different steps. When Jim Clarke sings out about shaking "your fat fanny," we can only guess what he meant; the actual dance, if there was one, is lost.

All stomps share a fast, danceable tempo. The rhythmic backbone is either $\frac{4}{4}$ or $\frac{4}{4}$ in cut-time, counted as $\frac{2}{4}$. With few exceptions the emphasis given to each beat is even—some musicians call it a "flat four" as opposed to a "syncopated four."

```
4/4:  1 2 3 4 / 1 2 3 4 / 1 2 3 4 / 1 2

         2   4     2   4     2   4     2
C      1   3   / 1   3   / 1   3   / 1
```

The flat four beat. Underlined numbers indicate emphasized beat.

Stomps generally follow the standard blues progression; none, to my knowledge, employ a one-chord, drone harmony like early barrelhouse pieces. However, subtle variations on the blues progression are not uncommon. *Big Fat Mama* is based on an unusual 10 bar form with a progression as follows:

measure :	1	2	3	4	5	6	7	8	9	10
	I	I	IV	IV	I	I	V^7	I	I-IV-I	V

Fat Fanny, a 24 bar stomp divided into two 12 bar sections, also contains a few harmonic oddities. In the first introductory chorus, the opening progression is:

F / D♭ / F / F . . .

The use of D♭ , which sounds almost like an F diminished chord, helps to build up harmonic anticipation that is finally resolved in the tonic (F major) at the end of the chorus. The second 12 bar section ends with a turnaround constructed along the same principle.

. . . F7 / Gm / Fm-D♭ -F-D♭ / F-D♭ / F :

The turnaround for *Fat Fanny Stomp*

The stomp is a sort of rural equivalent to boogie woogie. While it is unabashedly dance music, at times the stomp has been expanded into a personal statement, thus transcending its entertainment role. One of the most compelling examples is *Peetie Wheatstraw Stomp,* recorded in 1937 by Peetie Wheatstraw, the "Devil's Son-In-Law," one of the many pseudonyms used by William Bunch.

Bunch was born in 1902 in Ripley, Tennessee, but apparently spent most of his life around the infamous Deep Morgan and Valley districts of East St. Louis, Illinois. He first recorded in 1930 with a singer named Neckbones and the success of these early sides led to a prolific output of material—over eighty 78 rpm releases.

Judging from his records, Bunch was evidently a self-assured man who delighted audiences with his bravado. On *Shack Bully Stomp,* the last stomp he recorded, Wheatstraw's ego is riding high.

I used to play slow, but now I play it fast
I used to play slow, but now I play it fast
Just to see the women shake their yas, yas, yas.

Now I am a man that everybody knows
Now I am a man that everybody knows
And you can see a crowd everywhere he goes.

My name is Peetie, I'm on the line, you bet
My name is Peetie, I'm on the line, you bet
I got something new that I ain't never told you yet.

Froggie Blues offers some explicit advice in the same boastful style:

I am watching these men
That always grinning in my face (2x)
They don't mean me no good
They just wants to take my place.

Let me tell you men
How to keep your gal at home (2x)
Just put her to bed
And roll her all night long.

You hug her and kiss her
And squeeze her till she moans (2x)
Then stop and hypnotise her
And she sure won't leave home.

Liquor may have had a lot to do with his brave talk. Wheatstraw tells it this way in *Drinking Man Blues:*

The dealer asked me, "Peetie, how come you so rough?" (2x)
Well, now, I ain't bad, ooh, well, well
But I just been drinking that stuff.

That stuff will kill you
But it just won't quit (2x)
It will get you to the place, ooh, well, well
That you don't care who you hit.

It made me hit the policeman
And knock him off his feet (2x)
Takin' his pistol and his star, ooh, well, well
And walking up and down his beat.

On *Peetie Wheatstraw Stomp,* Bunch gives himself the additional title of "High Sheriff from Hell", as if to increase his already legendary stature.

Although Wheatstraw performed in an urban environment, the influence of rural styles is unmistakable. *Peetie Wheatstraw Stomp,* like rural barrelhouse numbers, has a repetitious structure; the same basic 12 bar chorus is used for each vocal line with few variations. The alternating bass line and simple harmonic constructions also indicate rural roots. The original Decca release of *Peetie Wheatstraw Stomp* has been reissued on *Blues Classics 4.*

Arthur "Montana" Taylor, a Westerner, as his name suggests, played piano stomps in the joints along Indiana Avenue in Indianapolis. His style reflects a strong boogie influence, reminiscent of Clarence Lofton and Cow Cow Davenport. In *Indiana Avenue Stomp,* the usual flat four stomp beat is replaced by a slightly syncopated one and the variations in Taylor's right hand solos indicate a sophisticated approach to the stomp. First recorded in 1929, *Indiana Avenue Stomp* is one of Taylor's best known compositions; it is currently available on Yazoo L-1028.

Jim Clarke's *Fat Fanny* and Walter Roland's *Big Fat Mama* are both delightful examples of the good-time stomp. They should be played in a spirited, off-hand manner, without self-consciousness. *Fat Fanny Stomp* is available on OJL 15 and *Big Fat Mama* on Yazoo L-1017.

Peetie Wheatstraw Stomp/*Peetie Wheatstraw*

by Peetie Wheatstraw

Fast

8va

1.

2.

Women all raving about Peetie Wheatstraw in this land
Women all raving about Peetie Wheatstraw in this land
He got some of these women, now, going from hand to hand.

Don't tell all the girls what that Peetie Wheatstraw do
Oooh, well . . . that Peetie Wheatstraw can do
That will throw suspicion, now, you know they will try him, too.

[Spoken] *Now play it a little bit, boy, let's see how it sounds.*

If you want to see the women that may clown
If you want to see the women lay down
Just let that Peetie Wheatstraw into your town.

I am Peetie Wheatstraw, the High Sheriff From Hell
I am Peetie Wheatstraw, the High Sheriff From Hell
The way I strut my stuff, oooh, well, now, you never can tell.

[Spoken] *Now do your stuff, Peetie.*

Indiana Avenue Stomp/*Montana Taylor*

by Montana Taylor

With a push

trem.

trem.

8va

8va

dim.

Fat Fanny Stomp/*Jim Clarke*

by Jim Clarke

1.
2.

[All lyrics spoken]

Now everybody get up off that thing and shake your fat fanny
When I say "ho" I mean shake your fat fanny. HO!
Shake your fat fanny, shake that thing, yeah, shake it.'
Do it, miss mama, do it.

When I say "ho" this time, I want everybody to walk into it
Walk into it like it's yours. HO!
Walk into it. Walk into it, juke boy.
That's what I'm talking 'bout. Do it, gal.

When I say "ho" this time, I want everybody to snatch it on back
Bring it, boy, snatch it on back. HO!
Snatch it back, snatch it on back, break it, boy.
Snatch it, snatch it to him.

When I say "ho" this time, I want everybody to gut it
Gut that thing. I mean gut it. HO!
Oh, gut it, Gut it gully low. Gut it like it live.
Mr. Juke boy, you're sure gutting that thing.

When I say "ho" this time, I want everybody to get up off it once more
And shake your fat fanny. HO!
Aw, shake your fat fanny. I mean shake your fanny.
Twirl that thing, gal, twirl it. Ring it and twist it a little bit. One more time.

When I say "ho" this time, I want everybody to Sally Long. HO!
Aw, Sally Long; Sally Long your fanny, gal. Sally that thing.
Sally it, shake your fat fanny. That's what I'm talking about.

Big Fat Mama/*Walter Roland*

by Walter Roland, W.R. Calaway and Clarence Williams

2.
Call - ing hey big ma - ma
call - ing
hey big ma - ma
call - ing hey big ma - ma
call - ing hey big ma - ma, Take your big legs off of me.
3.
She got
4.

She got great big legs, she got the walking size
She got great big legs, walking size
She got great big legs, walking size
And every time she leave me, you know it makes me cry.

Every time she call me, you know she makes me mad
Every time she call me, you know it makes me mad
Every time she call me, you know it makes me mad
But I ain't never told her about that man she had.

Boogie Woogie

What they call 'boogie woogie' now, we used to call 'dudlow joe' before it got famous.

–Little Brother Montgomery

When Clarence "Pine Top" Smith, a Chicago rent house party pianist, cut his *Pine Top's Boogie Woogie* in December, 1928, it crystalized the public's interest in boogie woogie for the first time. Hundreds of pianists, including Count Basie, Albert Ammons and Clarence Lofton, remade the song, and popular music imitators quickly capitalized on its success. Clarence Smith coined the term boogie woogie to describe his syncopated chordal bass figures and the wiggly dancing that the music inspired. Elements of boogie woogie had appeared on record a few years earlier. In the mid-1920's Cow Cow Davenport experimented with loosely syncopated boogie beats in his barrelhouse song forms and Meade Lux Lewis recorded his masterpiece, *Honky Tonk Train,* in 1927, a year before Pine Top entered a studio.

However, it was the commercial potential of *Pine Top's Boogie Woogie* that jolted the music business into a frantic search for the fast buck. Thousands of sheet music arrangements heralded the new style, but these were not exact transcriptions of the recordings; rather, efforts were made to simplify the sound by highlighting cliches and reducing the notation until it barely resembled the original songs. The buyers of this sheet music had a faddish interest in boogie woogie, so the superficial arrangements were accepted with few grumbles. There were some exceptions: Leeds Music put out a series, edited by Frank Paparelli, that accurately covered the fundamentals; and Leeds also published a few transcriptions, including Jimmy Yancey's *East St. Louis Blues, Roll 'Em Pete* by Pete Johnson and Pine Top Smith's version of *Jump Steady Blues.* Smith, incidently, was not destined to enjoy the success of his music; a few months after recording *Nobody Knows You When You're Down And Out* in 1929, he was shot to death during an argument at a party.

The selling of the blues actually dates back to Memphis when W.C. Handy first realized that blues had commercial value. After his success playing for the 1909 Crump mayoralty campaign, (Crump was a well-known politician), Handy knew he had a potential hit with *Mr. Crump,* but since no reputable publisher of popular music would even look at blues, Handy was forced to publish the song himself, without the benefit of any previous experience. As a result, Handy was badly burned on his first try; he was fooled into signing away his copyright to two unscrupulous promoters who took the song secretly to New York where it sold quite well. But Handy bounced back with more compositions like *St. Louis Blues,* and soon his Pace and Handy Music Publishing Company was doing a brisk business. As the blues craze swept the country following Mamie Smith's first recordings in 1920, the commercial possibilities became obvious to all. The blues was now show business, which in many respects was a disadvantage, for the public was exposed to only the grossest commercial exaggerations of the music, leaving the fresh, vital examples to be "rediscovered" by another generation.

Boogie woogie shared this unfortunate fate. By the 1940's, crass and unimaginative songs replaced much of what had once been an innovative piano style. Joe Davis Publishers of New York, for example, distributed a tasteless arrangement of classical music and boogie woogie, releasing such titles as *Boogie for the Widow* (based on *Merry Widow Waltz*) and *Boogie A La Minuet* (adapted from Beethoven's *Minuet in G*).

Boogie woogie, in its purer noncommercialized forms, is an instrumental solo style combining elements of blues and jazz. It's interesting to note that most blues music discographies consider boogie woogie and ragtime artists as *jazz* musicians and either omit their recordings altogether or list only a few early sessions before the "jazz" influence became too pronounced. Jazz discographies are no less ambiguous, sometimes claiming Jelly Roll Morton and James P. Johnson but rejecting Meade Lux Lewis.

Since boogie woogie is an instrumental solo style, it does not feature a vocal, the traditional focus of rural blues. The solo improvizatory technique is of primary importance, as in jazz styles, and, accordingly, boogie woogie pianists have often turned to jazz idioms for inspiration. From blues, boogie woogie borrowed its structure—the standard 12 bar progression—and its unique tonality, expressed on the keyboard with slurs and blues grace notes.

Boogie woogie improvizations are derived from simple riffs that are embellished in chorus after chorus. Take this example:

By manipulating the intervals and altering the rhythm, this phrase can be "improvized" into a continuous melody.

Eventually a complete solo line evolves by incorporating other melody fragments.

Boogie woogie developed principally in mid-Western urban centers—Chicago, Kansas City, Detroit, Cleveland—although the roots of the music go back to the rural South. Many cities had their "boogie schools," but the one in Chicago deserved the title of "university." Clarence Lofton, Jimmy Yancey, Doug Suggs and other veterans held forth every weekend at countless house parties, trading unwritten musical theories. Under their influence, a younger group of pianists, led by Meade Lux Lewis and Albert Ammons, eventually transformed boogie woogie into a concert music (that is, it transcended its original function as a dance music to become a listening music).

Lewis and Ammons made a tight boogie woogie duo. They lived in the same Chicago tenement (also shared for a time by Pine Top Smith), worked for the same taxi cab company by day, and practiced boogies at night. Lewis was twenty-two in 1927, when he recorded *Honky Tonk Train,* but it wasn't until 1939, when he was introduced at Cafe Society in New York, that his music began to pay off financially. Ammons, naturally, was discovered in New York at the same time.

The music of Meade Lux Lewis typifies the energetic technique and solo approach of the boogie woogie movement. *Honky Tonk Train* takes its form from the long tradition of guitar blues based on the locomotive; the monotonous left hand suggests the chugging of a train, while the right hand imitates whistles, honks and miscellaneous railroad noises. The piece may be simplified at first by ignoring the grace notes until a comfortable tempo, almost self-propelling, is achieved. The original Paramount recording of *Honky Tonk Train* has been reissued on Folkways 2810.

Modern Boogie Woogie

Although boogie woogie was suffocated by commercialism during the 1940's, in backalleys and juke joints the music continued to flourish. Memphis Slim and Dave Alexander are two fine artists who still use boogie woogie as the basis for their improvizations and song ideas.

Alexander, who grew up in rural Texas, learned about boogie woogie from the radio. "All the things I ever heard that I liked was on piano. Around 1945 I really started gettin' interested in playing, and finally we got a radio. This program came out of Tennessee—Randy's Record Show—and they played Albert Ammons' *Swanee River Boogie* as a theme song every night." In 1952, at the age of fourteen, Alexander started playing on the house party circuit. He only knew two or three boogies, but people paid him in food, liquor and possibly seventy-five cents a night. As he mastered the trade of the traveling piano player, Alexander's repertoire expanded—at first, to basic boogie woogie patterns and a few standards, and then, with increasing sophistication, to jazz tunes and ballads. Today Alexander lives and plays in San Francisco.

I Need a Little Spirit is based on a common bass line, the same one that Jimmy Yancey used in his *Stomp*, which is repeated without variation throughout the piece. The right hand is therefore free to explore a wide range of melodic ideas. Alexander fuses boogie woogie together with funky jazz riffs and harmonies to create a modern boogie style. *I Need a Little Spirit* is available on Arhoolie 1067.

Like Alexander, who learned boogie woogie in the rural joints of Texas, Peter Chatman received a similar folk education in Memphis, Tennessee, where he was born in 1916. In 1939 Chatman hopped a "late freight" train for Chicago, and soon afterwards recorded his first blues using the pseudonym Memphis Slim. His style displays a dazzling technical ability, but underneath Slim's sophisticated playing are the deep rural roots of barrelhouse piano.

Sail On Blues is based in the key of C minor, although Slim's ambivalent treatment of the third intervals (C-E and C-E♭) gives the piece a major sound at times. For example, in the 3rd measure of the first chorus, a minor third (E♭) grace note is attached to the major third, creating an overall major sound. Two bars later, however, the E♭–G tremelo sounds definitely minor. *Sail On Blues* was recorded in 1959 for Folkways Records and has been released on Folkways 3524.

Texas Boogie Woogie

In urban areas of the South, boogie woogie evolved with its own distinctive variations. Some of the most important regional developments took place in Texas, in the black sections of Houston, Dallas, San Antonio and Austin. Texas boogie woogie combined aspects of Texas barrelhouse (see *The Cows* by Robert Shaw) and rhythm and blues influences, yielding a relaxed, less stylized music than that heard up North.

Alex Moore has lived in Dallas all his life, traveling from the Deep Ellum section to other parts of the city, like Froggy Bottom, once a pit of crumbled buildings. Before "urban renewal" hit Dallas after World War II, legendary bluesmen wandered the streets playing in distinctive rural styles—Blind Lemon Jefferson, Leadbelly and Rambling Thomas. But as the area developed, as the shacks and joints were cleared away for shopping centers and expressways, these street singers moved on. The scene became more and more urbanized, and gradually the barrelhouse gave way to the boogie bar, the stomping grounds for men like Moore, Mercy Dee, Black Ace and Thunder Smith.

Whistlin' Alex Moore's Blues, so named for Moore's exceptional whistling ability, displays a full right hand solo style contrasted with a single note and chordal bass line. Note the abrupt transition as Moore moves from a repetitious boogie woogie figure to the alternating bass, common in barrelhouse compositions.

Chordal bass in *Whistlin' Alex Moore's Blues*

Alternating bass in *Whistlin' Alex Moore's Blues*

Moore's Blues can be heard on Arhoolie 1008.

Honky Tonk Train/*Meade Lux Lewis*

by Meade Lux Lewis

2nd Chorus
3

3rd Chorus
8va
trem.
5
3
3
3
3
3
3
3
3
3
3
3
rit.

Sail On Blues/*Memphis Slim*

by Memphis Slim

2nd Chorus

I Need a Little Spirit/*Dave Alexander*

by Dave Alexander as heard on Arhoolie LP 1067

2nd Chorus
trem.
trem.
trem.
trem.
8va

3rd Chorus:

8va

8va
rit.

Whistlin' Alex Moore's Blues/*Alex Moore*

Moderately

by Alex Moore

2nd Chorus
8va
trem.
gliss.
trem.

3rd Chorus
trem.
trem.
tighten up . . .
8va
3

4th Chorus
8va
8va
8va
trem.
gliss.
gliss.
rit.

Roll and Tumble

I stayed down in the midnight district a little while to learn about the blues; pianos are there; that's why it's called roll-houses, honky tonks.

—Sunnyland Slim

Our knowledge of blues piano is incomplete because, during certain periods, the music was not preserved. Commercial recordings began in the 1920's in the blues field and have provided a vast amount of material, but in order to recreate music played prior to that time, we must rely on older pianists who remember earlier styles. Going back to the birth of barrelhouse in the late 19th century is even more difficult—our knowledge is based on fragile memories, a few pieces of sheet music, and the descriptions of casual observers. Most vexing of all is the period from 1942 to 1946, when a ban on recording brought the industry to a near standstill. After World War II, a new style of blues piano emerged on the urban scene, a style which I call *roll and tumble,* but little is known about the beginnings of this tradition because so few recordings were made during the war.

This chapter is an informal reconstruction of how roll and tumble piano may have evolved from earlier barrelhouse and boogie styles. The four musicians discussed here—Sunnyland Slim, Black Boy Shine, Robert Shaw and Piano Red—have very little in common. They lived in different places, played in different styles, sang different songs. Yet by imaginatively filling in some of the unknown spaces, we can see a continuous line of development from "pure" barrelhouse to city roll and tumble.

Blacks immigrated from South to North mainly for economic reasons, as Sunnyland Slim explains from his own experience:

> *Missouri was a better state than Mississippi and Arkansas, so all the peoples in the South started leaving for Chicago 'cause you could earn 100, 150 times as much a year as in Arkansas. See, that's what started everybody going up to Missouri, and then on to Chicago. That's also what started people driftin'.*

The population shift coincided with the war-time boom in Northern states as industry, recovering from the Depression, bid up wages to find new workers. As blacks migrated, they brought their music with them, but unlike the urbanized blacks who played the city blues in the 1930's, these new arrivals had a distinctly rural perspective. Sunnyland Slim put it to me this way:

> *When I went into Chicago I had a country name—you know how it is—so there was no gettin' no bookings, no blues. I don't know if I was there a week, when Sonny Boy (Williamson) come in town; that's when me and Sonny Boy really got tight. We wouldn't play for no joints 'cause union scale was only 'bout $8.50 a night. So we started running around to people's houses—just a harp and piano—you earn more money that way. So me and Sonny Boy laid around and played and played.*

Aside from rent house parties, other institutions developed which satisfied the needs of the rural arrivals. Social gatherings with good, down-home cooking were an important forum for bluesmen, and Sunnyland Slim frequented many of them.

We'd have what's called a Blue Monday—chitlin's, turkey (I didn't go for turkey too much.) All get together and play: me, Big Bill, Roosevelt Sykes. And some of them wouldn't have no money by the time Monday come, so we put a pot out.

Social gatherings, rent house parties and the Northern experience all molded the rural barrelhouse styles. Another major factor was technological: the introduction of electrified musical instruments where there had previously been a completely acoustical sound. Although other instruments were amplified (e.g., the guitar, harmonica and voice) the piano usually was not, due to technical problems. It is difficult for microphones to pick up the entire range of the piano and even more difficult for small, inexpensive amplifiers to carry that sound without severe distortions. Thus, the piano player had to make adjustments—he had to be heard without amplification and he had to blend in with the new electrified sound. In addition, earlier piano styles were mostly *solo* performances. With the advent of amplified sound, blues bands became more popular, so the pianists also accommodated themselves to ensemble playing.

These developments took roughly ten years, from 1940 to 1950, and during most of that time shellac rationing and the Petrillo ban on recording limited the number of blues releases. Shellac rationing was necessary because of the dislocations of the war-time economy in 1941-42. This affected all recording activity. The Petrillo ban had an even more pervasive effect on blues records, for rather ironic reasons. In 1942 J.C. Petrillo, then the president of the powerful American Federation of Musicians, became so concerned about the deteriorating status of musicians that he announced a ban on all recording. His reasoning, uninformed at best, was that juke boxes were taking money away from "live" performances, therefore, making records for juke boxes was counterproductive for musicians. The ban lasted only two years, until 1944, but the effect was devastating.

In the space of a few years, recording giants like Columbia, Victor and Paramount had lost touch with the blues buying public. By 1950, all the major companies had left the blues field in one way or another, and the void was filled by small, independent firms like Chess, Vee Jay, Kent, King and a host of obscure labels like Tempo Tone, Hytone, Sunny, Fame and Swing Time. It was a discographer's nightmare, and during this confusing period, roll and tumble piano playing evolved and became a part of the post-war blues scene.

To reconstruct the beginnings of roll and tumble blues, let's go back to rural barrelhouse blues. Robert Shaw, born in Stafford, Texas in 1908, still plays in the rough style reminiscent of whiskey shacks. Today Shaw is a successful businessman in Austin and his prosperity has helped to preserve his music. When the bottom dropped out of the blues market during the Depression, Shaw "retired" but continued to play his songs in private. As a result, they have changed little; the version of *The Cows* in this book is much the same as versions played in backcountry barrelhouses in the 1920's.

The most striking thing about *The Cows* is its form-free, unorthodox and unpredictable. The chorus length is 13 measures and the "breaks"—moments when the left hand stops and the right hand fills in with a short solo—occur at different parts of the progression and for varying lengths of time. All in all, *The Cows,* as performed by Robert Shaw, would be a difficult, if not impossible, composition to play with a band. Its unsolidified format epitomizes the individualistic barrelhouse tradition. The original recording is available on Arhoolie.

As barrelhouse styles developed, some of the more sophisticated players became accompanists for blues singers. In many cases, they had to master new chords and a new musical vocabulary. Sunnyland Slim tells of one of his first ensemble experiences with the formidable Ma Rainey, the woman who taught Bessie Smith how to sing.

> *One time Ma Rainey didn't have no piano player to play. She called me; she had heard about me. When Ma Rainey was singing, she'd say, "Go back to B flat"–I didn't know but G, C and F–she said B flat. I'd just try and catch her voice. So I went to Memphis Slim; he had these facts [about chords] all in his head. And I get me a pint of whiskey (Slim love whiskey) and talk to him and learn the chords. So I got hip a little bit; I got hip from Slim.*

Other piano players like Roosevelt Sykes and Little Brother Montgomery developed great versatility and were capable of playing everything from popular ballads to gospel music.

Sugarland Blues is a good example of sophisticated barrelhouse, the kind that emerged from ensemble experiences and the interchange of ideas with other musicians. *Sugarland* was recorded by Black Boy Shine, the pseudonym used by Harold Holiday, in 1936. Holiday only recorded from 1935 to 1937; his first recordings were duets with Funny Paper Smith, a Texas guitarist, and his compositions reflect a knowledge of ensemble technique.

Unlike the rambling style of *The Cows, Sugarland Blues* is tightly constructed around a 12 bar form. The progression for the vocal line suggests influences from the so-called classic blues singers who used modulations and substitution chords.

G / G dim / G / G / C / E♭ / G / G / D7 / C♯ dim / G / D♭6 /

Progression for vocal chorus of *Sugarland Blues*

The original Vocalion 78 of *Sugarland Blues* has been reissued on Blues Classics 7.

Beginning in the early 1940's, piano players introduced rhythmic instruments into the rural barrelhouse style, usually by adding drums and a bass. During the 1950's, this trend, called "rhythm and blues", was developed in countless bands, including groups led by Fats Waller, Joe Liggins, Mercy Dee and Charles Brown. Many of these bands featured polished arrangements, but Willie Perryman was one musician who retained the raw texture of barrelhouse music in a rhythm and blues setting. Born in 1913, Perryman was inspired by the success of his older brother, Speckled Red, and traveled through the rent house party circuit seeking work. In 1950 Perryman recorded *Rockin' With Red* with a trio (piano, bass and drums) and this song launched a long recording career, first under the name Piano Red and later as Dr. Feelgood.

Piano Red's style is relatively simple. *Atlanta Bounce* uses few complex chords and a repetitious alternating bass. In many respects, *Atlanta Bounce* is a "modernized" version of the old barrelhouse stomp. Piano Red's ensemble arrangements are a natural extension of his solo style: the bass and drums support his bouncy left hand while his melodic material stays within a limited framework. Arhoolie Records has released *Atlanta Bounce* on 1064.

Roll and tumble piano is the culmination of several barrelhouse traditions: the pure, idiosyncratic style of Robert Shaw; the more sophisticated barrelhouse of

Black Boy Shine; and the "r&b" barrelhouse of Willy Perryman. Sunnyland Slim is one of several bluesmen who pioneered the roll and tumble sound that retained rural roots yet was tailored for an urban environment and the technology of amplification.

In roll and tumble playing, the left hand became progressively more boogie oriented; the alternating basses all but disappeared. However, the technical wizardry of boogie woogie does not dominate Sunnyland's playing. Instead his songs feature full vocal lines that are as important as the piano. In 1953 Sunnyland and guitarist Leroy Foster recorded *Roll, Tumble And Slip,* a blues that epitomized the emerging style. The song was released on the obscure Opera label, with Sunnyland using the name Delta Joe, a direct reference to his roots in the Mississippi Delta region.

Mama, I rolled and I tumbled baby
And I cried the whole night long
Darlin', you know I rolled this morning
I did not know right from wrong.

It's you Baby, although recorded over a decade later, illustrates the same roll and tumble technique. The left hand figures are taken from boogie riffs, yet the variations reveal the loose interpretation of rural barrelhouse piano:

Note the glissandi and walking bass lines mixed in with traditional boogie figures. *It's You Baby* is available on Storyville 671 169.

Robert Shaw

The Cows/*Robert Shaw*

by Robert Shaw

8va
8va

1.
D. S.
2.

Sugarland Blues/*Black Boy Shine*

by Black Boy Shine

nev-er have noth-ing long as you live in su-gar-land
You'll
nev-er have noth-ing long as you live in su-gar-land.
Be-cause you're work-in' for a wom-an and a sweet black man.
1.
I dumped
2.
rit.

I dumped sugar all day
Clean until broad daylight
I dumped sugar all day
Clean until broad daylight
I done everything for that woman
Still she don't treat me right.

I'm gonna stop working, baby
Get yourself another man
I'm gonna stop working, baby
Get yourself another man
Cause I've got another woman
You'll have to do the best you can.

I worked for you in the winter
I worked for you in the ice and snow
I worked for you in the winter
Worked for you in the ice and snow
Then baby you told me
You didn't want me no more.

It done come summertime and
I ain't gonna work no more
It done come summertime
I ain't gonna work no more
Because I've found another woman
Baby and I'm gonna let you go.

Atlanta Bounce/*Piano Red*

by Piano Red

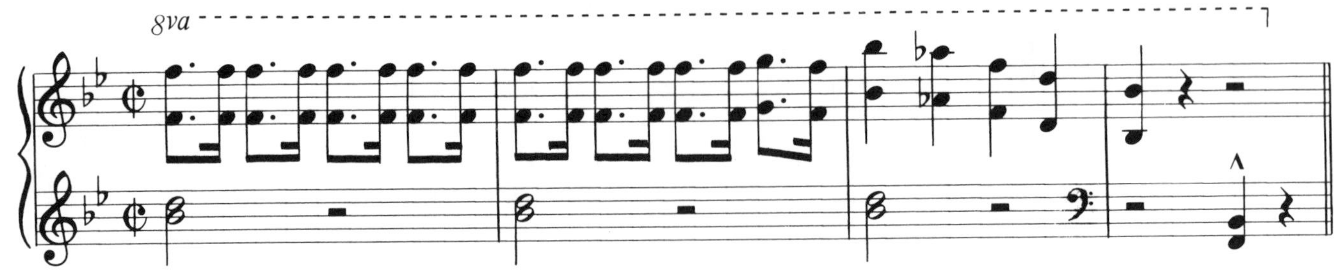

3rd Chorus
4th Chorus
rit.

It's You Baby/*Sunnyland Slim*

by Albert Luandrew (Sunnyland Slim)

Well I
To Coda:
might - a loved you ba - by
To Coda:
wom - an I won't fool a - round with you no more
D. S.
2. Well it's
D. S.
Coda:
Oh I hates to be a - lone.
Coda:
trem.

Well it's you
You know you got me ringing my hands and crying
Woooo . . .
You got me ringing my hands and crying
Well I found out lately, baby
Mama, to me you been on the line.

Well it's you
Got me doing things on the floor
Well it's you little girl
Got me doing things on the floor
You know I love you baby
It's better if you just go along.

[Spoken] *Oh, yeah!*

Well it's you
Cause me to leave my happy home
Oooooh . . .
You cause me to leave my happy home
Well I try to love you baby
Oh! I hates to be alone.

Sunnyland Slim

Barrelhouse Blues

The old dirty tone is barrelhouse blues. To get that, pad the piano strings with old newspapers or some burlap bag and kick the front board hard for rhythm. Don't care how it looks, just attention how it sounds. They don't make pianos like that no more.

—Jelly Roll Morton

Just as stomps and boogies made people dance, slower barrelhouse blues became the forum for personal observations about life. Freedom, rootlessness, women, death—these topics recur frequently in the repertoires of itinerant bluesmen and give us an idea of what their worlds were like.

Views about women were affected by feelings of rootlessness. Constant mobility made a normal domestic life nearly impossible, and infidelity was more or less accepted on the barrelhouse circuit. Nevertheless, many bluesmen still yearned for the old-fashioned values of a domestic existence. In *I Can Tell By the Way You Smell,* Walter Davis sets forth, in a humorous, pithy manner, his views on what is socially acceptable. "You been doing something wrong," he says after listing several indiscretions. One thing that Davis really draws the line on is a woman "showing her linen" to any man. "That's something that I just can't stand," he warns.

I Can Tell has an unsyncopated walking bass line, similar in style to the basses of Cow Cow Davenport, Leroy Carr, and Cripple Clarence Lofton. Davis also uses a minimum of chordal harmonies, which gives his blues a primitive, one-chord sound. In this respect, the piece resembles the music of Romeo Nelson. *I Can Tell By the Way You Smell* is available on Yazoo 1025.

In *Long Lonesome Day,* Jesse James describes the emptiness of his nomadic life by commenting, "I been to the nation, 'round the territo, but I found no heaven on earth; Lord, no where I go." Then, as if to equate this emptiness with the horror of imprisonment, James mentions his experience at the "Big House," the penitentiary. In an ambivalent phrase, sorrowful yet cavalier, he says that he "don't even care" if he gets the chair. (Leroy Carr, another pianist, approached this predicament with a different line. In *Take a Walk Around the Corner,* Carr sings, "Well, it's please, please, please, don't send me to the electric chair/Just give me my time and I'll try to do it anywhere.")

The 24 bar chorus of *Long Lonesome Day* is divided into two sections—8 and 16 bars respectively—by a distinctive change in the bass line. From a chordal "flat four" bass, James abruptly shifts to a "doubled-up" walking bass in the second 16 bar section.

First bass pattern

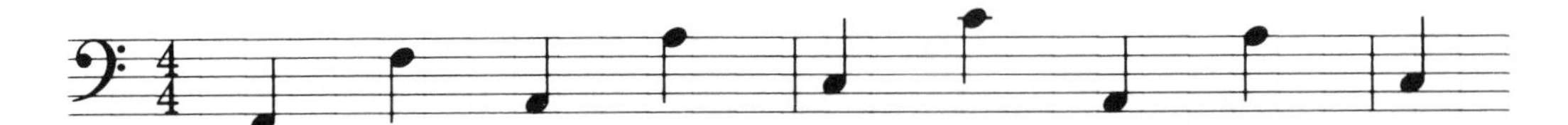

Second bass pattern

After James recorded this blues for Decca at their Chicago studio, the original tape of the session was evidently speeded up so that the song sounds as if it were performed in the key of D♭ major. In my transcription, I transposed the piece to C major (which I believe was the original key and is certainly more manageable than the five flats of D♭ .) *Long Lonesome Day* has been reissued on OJL 15.

Fast numbers often rely on rhythmic excitement to hold the listeners interest, but for slower tempos, harmonic variation is necessary. One common device for adding harmonic richness is the use of 10ths in the bass line. This allows for melodic passing tones and unusual chord voicings. In *Short Haired Blues* by Kid Stormy Weather, 10ths descent "through" a C major triad, giving the opening progression an interesting dissonance.

C - C6 - C - D#° 6♭9 / C9^{11} - G7 - G6 - G7 / C . . .

Introductory progression to *Short Haired Blues*

Dink Johnson plays 10ths to achieve a full-sounding accompaniment for the delicate melodic lines of *Stella Blues.* He also adds rhythmic interest by changing from 10ths to a modified boogie bass in the second chorus. This is similar to the bass line transition in *Long Lonesome Day. Stella Blues* is available on Storyville 671 155, and Blues Classics has reissued *Short Haired Blues* on BC 7.

Lonesome Day Blues/*Jesse James*

by Jesse James

Last time
to Coda

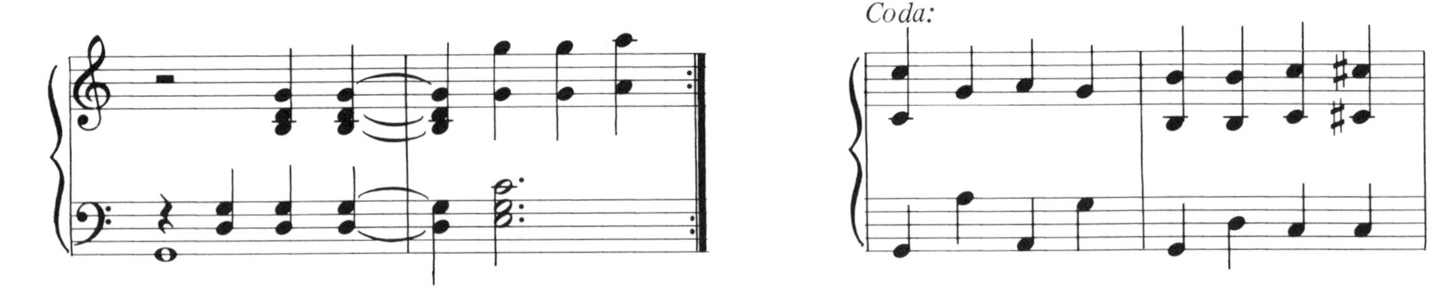

Coda:

I been to the nation, 'round the territo
You hear me talking to ya, you got to reap what you sow
I been all through the nation and 'round the territo
But I found no heaven on earth; Lord no where I go.

I'm going to the Big House and I don't even care
Don't you hear me talking to 'em, scolding to my death
I'm going home and I don't even care
I might get four, five years; Lord and I might get the chair.

Owls stop and listen, see the morning rain
You hear me talking 'till you started praying
You better stop by 'n listen and see what the morning bring
It might bring you sunshine; Lord and it may bring rain.

Some got six months, some got a solid year
You hear me talking to ya, but what made you stop by here
Some of them got six months, partner, and some got a solid year
But I believe my partner; Lord got lifetime here.

I Can Tell By the Way You Smell/*Walter Davis*

by Walter Davis

You show your linen to any man
And that's something, mama, that I just can't stand.

Chorus:
You been doing something wrong
Doing something wrong

You been doing something wrong
I can tell by the way you smell.

Here you come walking just like a goose
You look like somebody just turned you loose.

Chorus

He got the motion and she got the swing
Look at papa out there on that thing.

Chorus

Stella Blues/*Dink Johnson*

by Oliver (Dink) Johnson

tr
ritard.

Short Haired Blues/*Kid Stormy Weather*

by Kid Stormy Weather

That's all right ba - by,
that is all right for you.
That's all right ba - by,
Lord, for the way you do.
1.
1.

2.
16va
trem.
16va
trem.
15va
8va
3
D. S.

3.
8va
8va
8va
3

The blues came down my alley
Rolling up into my back door
The blues came down my alley
Rolling up into my back door
I got the blues this morning
Lord, Lord like I never had before.

Mama remember the time
Babe I made you like it and how
Yeah, mama remember the time
Babe I made you like it and how
But the things you trying to do
Babe, somebody's doing it now.

Gone old black gal
You know you can't make me change
Say, gone old black gal
You know you can't make me change
Cause you hair is so short
Swear to God I can smell your brains.

Way, way down babe
Way down in old polock town
Now way, way down babe
Way down in old polock town
There the roaches and the pimps, babe
Done tore my little gin house down.

Exercises

COORDINATION

The problem of coordinating the right and left hands in barrelhouse and boogie piano is two-fold. First, the hands must achieve a certain degree of independence; that is, the right hand must be able to play a varying rhythmic pattern without affecting the steadiness of the left hand. Second, the bass and melodic line must be integrated into a flowing, dynamic progression.

Exercises for independence

Exercises for integration

FINGERING

Unlike the prescribed world of classical piano, in blues, anything goes. In fact, many celebrated blues pianists with physical handicaps—One Arm Pike and the three-fingered Mamie Desdoumes are two colorful examples—were forced to create their own fingering method. These exercises outline some common fingering patterns for grace notes, slurs, and short riffs.

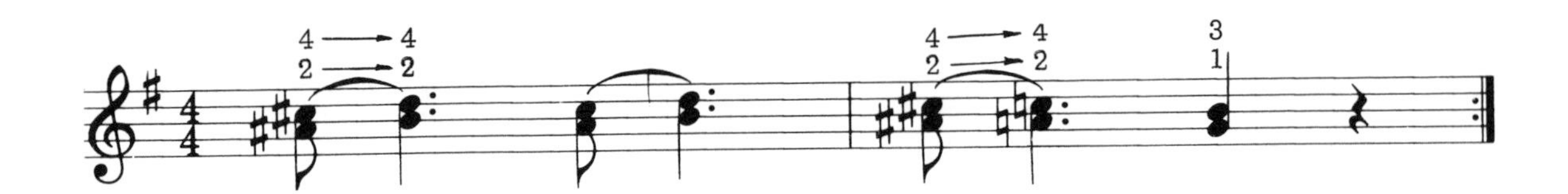

TREMOLO

The tremolo is a frequent device used in blues and should be practiced with a variety of boogie and barrelhouse bass lines [use the Appendix of bass lines] . This exercise is in the key of C major, but may be transposed to any key for a varied practice session.

Further Reading

Jelly Roll Morton—Blues, Stomps & Ragtime, Edwin H. Morris & Co., New York, 1960. Seventeen Morton compositions presented in their original copyrighted form which does not, unfortunately, accurately characterize the recordings.

Mister Jelly Roll by Alan Lomax, Grosset & Dunlap, New York, 1950. A classic music biography by a noted folklorist.

Sportin' House: New Orleans and the Jazz Story by Stephen Longstreet, Sherbourne Press, Los Angeles, 1965. A unique and spicy historical account of the infamous Storyville District and environs.

Leed's Eight to the Bar by Frank Paparelli, Leeds Music Corp., New York, 1941. Paparelli's book was one of the first serious musical explanations of boogie woogie. The seven boogie woogie "solos" included with the text, however, are not very instructive.

Jazz Dance: The Story of American Vernacular Dance by Marshall and Jean Stearns, Macmillan, New York, 1968. An intriguing history and analysis of American dance forms.

The Devil's Son-In-Law by Paul Garon, Studio Vista, London, 1971. Garon thoughtfully discusses Peetie Wheatstraw and his contemporaries. Now out of print due to the bankruptcy of the publishers.

Early Jazz by Gunther Schuller, Oxford University Press, New York, 1968. Schuller makes some perceptive comments about Morton's music in his rather dry, academic style.

Six Blues-Roots Pianists by Eric Kriss, Oak Publications, New York, 1973. Accurate transcriptions and discussion of six important pianists: Jimmy Yancey, Little Brother Montgomery, Champion Jack Dupree, Otis Spann, Speckled Red and Roosevelt Sykes.

Living Blues, P.O. Box 11303, Chicago, IL 60611. The best blues magazine published today, *Living Blues* features interviews, reviews, biographies, and some instructional material.

Blues Records: 1943-1966 by Mike Leadbitter and Neil Slaven, Oak Publications, New York, 1968. An encyclopedia of more than two decades of recorded blues. The only work of its kind.

Discography

PART I—BARRELHOUSE AND BOOGIE

This is a selected list of performances by the twenty-two artists discussed in this book. Only currently available albums have been listed and therefore many of the titles are reissues, not original labels. For more detailed discographical information and other recordings by these artists, consult *Blues and Gospel Records 1902-1942* by Dixon and Godrich (Storyville Publications), and *Blues Records 1943-1966* by Leadbitter and Slaven (Oak Publications).

Dave Alexander

Love Is Just For Fools, World Pacific WPS 21983/ March 7, 1969, Los Angeles
Good Soul Music
Highway 59
The Sky Is Crying, Arhoolie 1067/ July 31, 1972, Berkeley, Calif.
Lonesome Train Blues
Swanee River Boogie/August 1, 1972
I Need A Little Spirit
Good Home Cooking
The Rattler
There Ought To Be A Law
A Tribute To My Father
13 Is My Number
The Judgement
The Hoodoo Man, Arhoolie 1071/December 5, 1972, San Francisco
St. James Infirmary
Blue Tumbleweed
Sundown
Suffering With The Lowdown Blues
Strange Woman
Cold Feeling
Jimmy, Is That You?
So You Want To Be A Man
The Dirt On The Ground

Barrelhouse Buck (Thomas MacFarland)

I Got To Go Blues, Origin Jazz Library OJL 20/ August 10, 1934, Chicago
Lieutenant Blues, Folkways FG 3554/ May 12, 1961, Alton, Ill.
Alton Blues
Four O'Clock Blues
20th Street Blues
Mercy Blues
So Long Buck
I'm Going To Write You A Letter
Mary Ain't I Been One Good Man To You
Reminiscences
Make Me A Soldier Of The Cross
Nina Blues
Taylor Avenue Blues

Black Boy Shine (Harold Holiday)

Sugarland Blues, Blues Classics BC 7/ November 20, 1936, San Antonio, Tex.

Jim Clarke

Fat Fanny Stomp, Origin Jazz Library OJL 15/ December 1929, Chicago

Cow Cow Davenport (Charles Davenport)

Cow Cow Blues, Biograph BLP 1001Q/ April 1927 (piano roll), Cincinnati, Ohio
State Street Jive, Yazoo L-1028/July 16, 1928, Chicago
Alabama Strut, Origin Jazz Library OJL 15/ October 2, 1928, Chicago
Back In The Alley, Historical HLP 29/May 1, 1929, Chicago
Mooch Piddle

Walter Davis

M & O Blues no. 3, RBF 12/ February 10, 1932, Dallas, Tex.
Sloppy Drunk Again, Yazoo L-1015/February 25, 1935, Chicago
Sweet Sixteen, Mamlish S-3800
I Can Tell By The Way You Smell, Yazoo L-1025/ July 28, 1935, Chicago

Santa Claus
Jacksonville—Part 2/April 3, 1936, Chicago
Call Your Name/July 21, 1939, Chicago
Why Should I Be Blue?/July 12, 1940, Chicago
Please Don't Mistreat Me
Can't See Your Face

Jesse James

Southern Casey Jones, Blues Classics BC 5/
June 3, 1936, Chicago
Lonesome Day Blues, Origin Jazz Library OJL 15
Ramrod (Sweet Patuni), Yazoo L-1028

Dink Johnson

Las Vegas Stomp, Storyville 671 155/October 1947,
Los Angeles
Stella Blues

Kid Stormy Weather

Short Haired Blues, Blues Classics BC 7/
October 17, 1935, Jackson, Miss.

Meade Lux Lewis

Honky Tonk Train, Folkways FJ 2810/December 1927,
Chicago
Dupree Blues, Storyville SLP 183/October 1939,
Chicago
Special No. 1, Folkways FJ 2809/August 18, 1944,
New York
Glendale Glide, Storyville 671 155
Randini's Boogie

Cripple Clarence Lofton

Strut That Thing, Folkways FJ 2804/April 2, 1935,
Chicago
Monkey Man Blues, Yazoo L-1015
Brown Skin Girls, Yazoo L-1025 (also Blues
Classics BC 5)/July 18, 1935, Chicago
Pine Top's Boogie Woogie, Origin Jazz Library
OJL 15/1939, Chicago
Juke Joint Stomp, Yazoo L-1015/c. 1939, Chicago
I Don't Know (also Swaggie S1235)
State Street Blues
Change My Mind Blues
Streamline Train (also Swaggie S1235)
South Side Mess Around
Traveling Blues, Swaggie S1235/c. 1939, Chicago
Mistaken Blues
Pitchin' Boogie
Mercy Blues

Memphis Slim (Peter Chatman)

Walkin' The Boogie, Folkways FG 3524/
July 19, 1959, New York
Cow Cow Blues
Jefferson County Blues
Four O'Clock Blues
Mister Freddie
Trouble In Mind
44 Blues
88 Boogie
Sail On Blues
Down Home Blues
Down That Big Road
Roll And Tumble
Crowing Rooster
Woman Boogie Blues
The Bells, Folkways FG 3535/c. 1959, New York
The Lord Have Mercy On Me
My Baby Don't Love Me No More
I Left That Town
Boogie After Midnight
The Train Is Gone
Pine Top's Boogie
Whiskey Drinking Blues
San Juan Blues
In The Evening
How Long Blues
Sail On Little Girl
John Henry
El Capitan, Archive of Folk Music FS-215/
1960-61, Copenhagen, Denmark
This Is A Good Time To Write A Song
I'm So All Alone
True Love
Two Of A Kind
Big City Girl
Three And One Boogie
Bertha May
Celeste Boogie
Three Woman Blues

Alex Moore

Whistlin' Alex Moore's Blues, Arhoolie F1008/
July 30, 1960, Dallas, Tex.
Pretty Woman With A Sack Dress On
Rubber Tired Hack
You Say I Am A Bad Feller
From North Dallas To The East Side
Miss No-Good Weed
Black-Eyed Peas And Hog Jowls
Boogie In The Barrel
Going Back To Froggy Bottom
July Boogie
West Texas Woman

Frisky Gal
Wake Up Old Lady, Arhoolie F 1006
Chock House Boogie, Arhoolie F1017
Boogiein' In Strassburg, Arhoolie 1048/
October 23, 1969, Stuttgart, Germany
Alex Thinking
New Blue Bloomer Blues
Rock And Roll Bed Blues
Flossie Mae
Just A Blues
Rolling Around Dallas
Having Fun Here And There

Jelly Roll Morton

One-Step Medley No. 2, Biograph BLP 1001Q/
c. 1915 (piano roll), Chicago
Tom Cat Blues, Folkways FJ 2809/July 1924,
New York (?)
Mr. Jelly Roll, Biograph BLP 1004Q/September 1924
(piano roll), Cincinnati, Ohio
London Blues
Grandpa's Spells
Stratford Huntch
Shreveport Stomp
King Portor
Tin Roof Blues
The Jelly Roll Blues/November 1924 (piano roll),
Cincinnati, Ohio
Tom Cat Blues
Sweet Man/December 1925 (piano roll), Chicago
Midnight Mama/October 1926 (piano roll),
Chicago (?)
Dead Man Blues
Finger Buster, Historical HLP 29/December 1, 1938,
Washington D.C.
Creepy Feeling
Honky Tonk Music
Climax Rag/September 29, 1940, New York
Winin' Boy Blues/ July 14, 1940, New York (?)

Romeo Nelson

Head Rag Hop, Swaggie 33478/September 5, 1929,
Chicago
Gettin' Dirty Just Shakin' That Thing, Origin Jazz
Library OJL 15/October 9, 1929, Chicago
Dyin' Rider Blues, RBF 12/November 26, 1929, Chicago

Peetie Wheatstraw (William Bunch)

Mama's Advice, Blues Classics BC 4/November 4, 1930,
Chicago
C & A Blues, Origin Jazz Library OJL 20/
January 7, 1931, Chicago
Ice And Snow Blues, Blues Classics BC 4/
September 28, 1931, Chicago
Sleepless Nights Blues, Origin Jazz Library OJL 20/
March 17, 1932, New York
Throw Me In The Alley/August 24, 1934, Chicago
Good Woman Blues, RBF 12/February 13, 1936,
Chicago
Working Man, Blues Classics BC 4/February 18, 1936,
New York
Peetie Wheatstraw Stomp/March 26, 1937, Chicago
Peetie Wheatstraw Stomp No. 2
Working On The Project/March 30, 1937, Chicago
Shack Bully Stomp/April 1, 1938, New York
Road Tramp Blues

Piano Red (Willie Perryman)

Ten Cent Shot, Arhoolie 1064/May 7, 1972,
Macon, Ga.
Pushing That Thing
Atlanta Bounce
Red's How Long Blues
Corrina, Corrina
You Ain't Got A Chance
My Baby Left Me
Let's Get It On
Red's Boogie
Rockin' With Red
Wrong Yo-Yo

Walter Roland

T Model Blues, Yazoo L-1017/July 17, 1933,
New York
Jookit Jookit/July 19, 1933, New York
Early This Morning/July 20, 1934, New York
Dices' Blues, RBF 12/July 30, 1934, New York
Big Mama (Yazoo L-1017)/August 2, 1934,
New York [alternate title *Big Fat Mama*]
Penniless Blues, Yazoo L-1012/March 20, 1935,
New York

Robert Shaw

Whores Is Funky, Arhoolie F 1010/1963, Austin, Tex.
The Cows
Here I Come With My Dirty, Dirty Duckins On
The Clinton
Black Gal
Hattie Green
The Ma Grinder
People, People Blues
Put Me In The Alley
Piggly Wiggly Blues
Turn Loose My Tongue, Arhoolie F 1012

Sunnyland Slim (Albert Luandrew)

When I Was Young (tk 1), Biograph BLP 12010/
July 19, 1949, Chicago

When I Was Young (tk. 2)
Roll, Tumble And Slip, Muskadine 1/1953, Chicago
Prison Bound Blues, Storyville 671 196/
October 1964, Copenhagen, Denmark
Johnson Machine Gun
Miss Ida B.
Sad And Lonesome Blues
That's All Right
Anna Lou Blues
I Done You Wrong
It's You Baby
Tin Pan Alley
Brown Skin Woman
You're The One
Going Down Slow

Montana Taylor (Arthur Taylor)

Whoop & Holler Stomp, Historical HLP 29/
April 22, 1929, Chicago
Hayride Stomp
Indiana Avenue Stomp, Yazoo L-1028/April 23, 1929,
Chicago

Barrelhouse Welch (Nolan Welsh)

Dying Pickpocket Blues, Yazoo L-1028/
June 16, 1926, Chicago

PART II—SUGGESTED PIANO BLUES ALBUMS

This is a selected list of outstanding piano blues albums listed alphabetically by label name. I have tried to include only those recordings currently available from the issuing company or from specialty record stores. Consult the Appendix for the addresses of the companies mentioned in this list. Space permits only a brief description of each album.

Archive of Folk Music
FS 215 Memphis Slim
FS 216 Otis Spann
FS 217 Champion Jack Dupree

Arhoolie Records
F 1007 Mercy Dee
F 1008 Alex Moore
F 1010 Robert Shaw: Texas Barrelhouse Piano
F 1064 Piano Red
F 1067 Dave Alexander: The Rattler
F 1071 Dave Alexander: The Dirt On The Ground

Atlantic Blues Originals Series
7229 Chicago Piano, Vol. 1—Mama and Jimmy Yancey

Barnaby/Candid Series
Z 30246 Otis Spann Is The Blues

Biograph Records
BLP 12010 After Hour Blues—w/Little Brother Montgomery, St. Louis Jimmy and Sunnyland Slim
BLP 1001Q Parlor Piano—w/Cow Cow Davenport, James P. Johnson, Jelly Roll Morton, Fats Waller, others. Recorded from rare piano rolls, 1915-27.
BLP 1004Q Jelly Roll Morton: 1924-1926 Piano Rolls

Blues Classics
BC 4 Peetie Wheatstraw and Kokomo Arnold. Several excellent examples of Peetie's piano work.

Columbia Records
C 30496 Leroy Carr

Delmark Records
601 Dirty Dozens—Speckled Red's Barrelhouse Piano
607 Roosevelt Sykes: Hard Driving Blues
616 Roosevelt Sykes In Europe
626 Blues Piano Orgy—w/Speckled Red, Curtis Jones, Sunnyland Slim, Little Brother Montgomery, Roosevelt Sykes, Otis Spann. Superb sides by Little Brother including *Tremblin' Blues.*

Folkways Records
FJ 2809 Piano Jazz, Anthology no. 9—w/Jelly Roll Morton, Meade Lux Lewis, Jack Dupree, others.
FG 3524 The Real Boogie Woogie of Memphis Slim
FG 3527 Little Brother Montgomery Blues
FG 3535 Memphis Slim and the Real Honky Tonk
FG 3554 Barrelhouse Buck (Thomas MacFarland)
FG 3555 The Barrelhouse Blues of Speckled Red
FS 3825 The Woman Blues of Jack Dupree
FS 3827 Roosevelt Sykes: The Honeydripper
FTS 31014 Little Brother Montgomery

Historical Records
HLP 29 Hot Pianos 1926-40—w/Cow Cow Davenport, Montana Taylor, Jelly Roll Morton, Fats Waller.

Jazz Piano
JP 5003 Library of Congress Recordings of Albert Ammons, Pete Johnson and Meade Lux Lewis

Milestone Records
2003 The Immortal Jelly Roll Morton
2009 Boogie Woogie Rarities—w/Cripple Clarence Lofton, Wesley Wallace, Meade Lux Lewis, others.

Origin Jazz Library
OJL 15 Rugged Piano Classics—w/Cripple Clarence Lofton, Romeo Nelson, Jesse James, others.
OJL 20 The Blues in St. Louis—w/Peetie Wheatstraw, Speckled Red

RBF
RF 12 Piano Blues—w/Walter Roland, Wesley Wallace, Little Brother Montgomery, Roosevelt Sykes, others.

Storyville (Danish Import)
117 The Dirty Dozens—Speckled Red
155 Barrelhouse Blues and Boogie, Vol. 1—w/Jimmy Yancey Meade Lux Lewis, others
168 Piano Blues—w/Otis Spann, Speckled Red, others
169 Sunnyland Slim: Portraits In Blues, Vol. 8
183 Barrelhouse Blues and Boogie, Vol. 2—w/Jimmy Yancey, Pete Johnson, others
184 Boogie Woogie Trio—Albert Ammons, Meade Lux Lewis, Pete Johnson
189 Roosevelt Sykes: Portraits In Blues, Vol. 11
194 The Blues of Champion Jack Dupree
208 Barrelhouse Piano—Meade Lux Lewis

Swaggie Records (Australian Import)
S 1213 Jelly Roll Morton 1938-40
S 1235 Pitchin' Boogie—Jimmy Yancey and Cripple Clarence Lofton

Testament Records
2202 Jimmy Walker and Erwin Helfer: Rough And Ready

Yazoo Records
L-1015 Favorite Country Blues Piano-Guitar Duets—w/Charlie Spand, Cripple Clarence Lofton, Leroy Carr, others
L-1017 Walter Roland (and Lucille Bogan)
L-1025 Cripple Clarence Lofton and Walter Davis
L-1028 Barrelhouse Piano—w/Little Brother Montgomery Cow Cow Davenport, Barrelhouse Welch, others. Remarkable and rare sides.
L-1033 Roosevelt Sykes: The Country Blues Piano Ace. Important early recordings.

Appendix A—Barrelhouse and Boogie Bass Lines

DRONES

Common in early barrelhouse pieces and early boogies. Similar to one-chord guitar blues that use a continuous tonic tone; probably evolved around the same time (c. 1890's). Great rhythmic variety; the Dupree excerpt is in an early boogie style, while the Sykes excerpt has a much looser structure. Romeo Nelson example combines drones and glissandos (see Glissando reference below).

Romeo Nelson, *Dyin' Rider*

Champion Jack Dupree, *Too Evil To Cry*

Roosevelt Sykes, *Highway 61 Blues*

SIMPLE ALTERNATING BASSES

A further evolution in drone basses employing octaves and open fifths. The Lofton and Speckled Red excerpts show hints of boogie woogie. Harmonic combinations are usually limited to the notes of the basic triad. Widely played in barrelhouses from the turn of the century to the late twenties.

Barrelhouse Welch, *Dying Pickpocket Blues*

Speckled Red, *Cow Cow Blues*

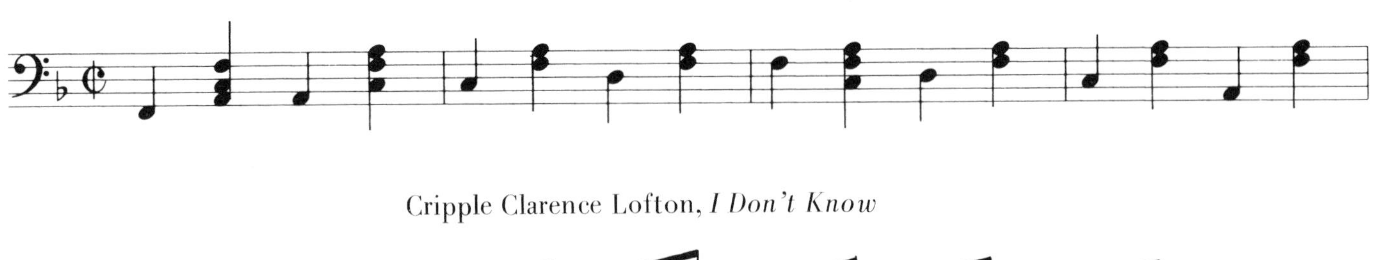

Cripple Clarence Lofton, *I Don't Know*

Piano Red (Willie Perryman), *Rockin' With Red*

COMPLEX ALTERNATING BASSES

Greater harmonic role with use of passing tones, chord inversions and doubling of octaves. Introduction of 7ths and 6ths in left hand. Used primarily in barrelhouse blues and stomps, although played a vital role in ragtime development, where further complexities were devised by Jelly Roll Morton, James P. Johnson, and earlier, by Scott Joplin.

Peetie Wheatstraw, *Peetie Wheatstraw Stomp*

Black Boy Shine, *Sugarland Blues*

Little Brother Montgomery, *Tremblin' Blues*

GLISSANDOS

A technique used mostly in rural barrelhouse styles, probably developed to imitate slides on the guitar. Primary notes outline a chord triad or walking bass line, with the glissandos added for rhythmic and harmonic interest. Adopted for use with other bass figures (cf. drones in Romeo Nelson's *Dyin' Rider*).

Jelly Roll Morton, *Jelly Roll Blues*

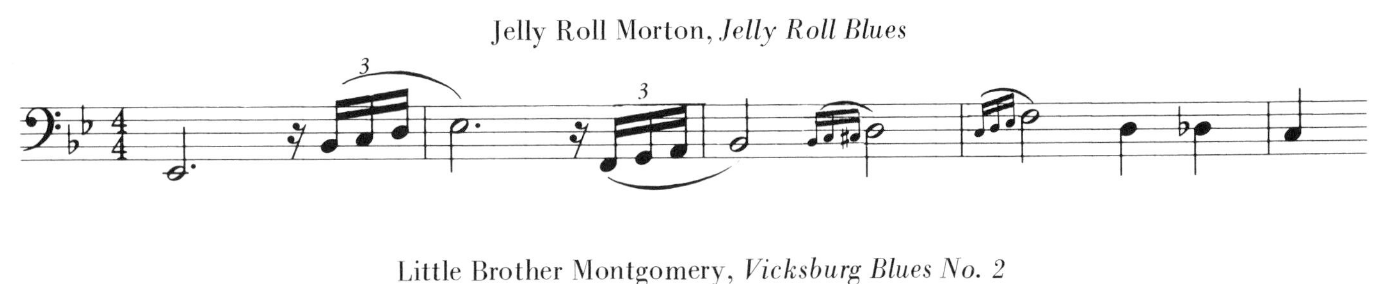

Little Brother Montgomery, *Vicksburg Blues No. 2*

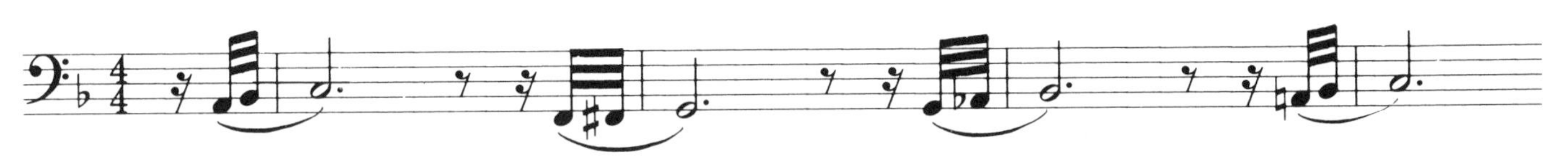

SINGLE NOTE BASSES

Simple accompaniments that emphasize the root and fifth of a chord. Used to support a dominant right hand and common in stomps and slow blues.

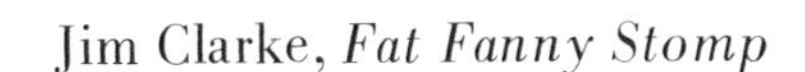

Jim Clarke, *Fat Fanny Stomp*

Walter Roland, *Big Fat Mama*

Roosevelt Sykes, *Red-Eye Jesse Bell*

WALKING BASSES

Borrowed and adapted from jazz musicians, these figures have a considerable range from simple chord arpeggios to sophisticated passing tones and modulations. Dotted eighth note riffs enjoyed wide boogie applications. Unsyncopated lines, like Davenport excerpt, were common in barrelhouse compositions.

Speckled Red, *Cow Cow Blues*

Cow Cow Davenport, *State Street Jive*

Leroy Carr, *Good Woman Blues*

10THS

For slow barrelhouse blues when a rhythmic left hand is not important. Became the foundation of popularized piano blues in the 1920's and also had successful jazz applications. Bessie Smith's piano players, for example, often used descending 10ths in their blues accompaniments even when backing up jazz soloists.

Dink Johnson, *Stella Blues*

Kid Stormy Weather, *Short Haired Blues*

BOOGIE WOOGIE: CHORDAL

Used with single note right hand solos. Favored for rhythmic dance numbers requiring loud volume and little melodic variety. The cornerstone of the boogie woogie style.

Meade Lux Lewis, *Honky Tonk Train*

Memphis Slim, *Sail On Blues*

Clarence Smith, *Pine Top's Boogie Woogie*

BOOGIE WOOGIE: SINGLE NOTE

Increased melodic and harmonic role. Incorporated elements of walking basses. Frequent use of major and minor thirds, sixths, sevenths, and passing tones. Most examples employ dotted eighth-note rhythms.

Dave Alexander, *I Need A Little Spirit*

Jimmy Yancey, *Yancey's Bugle Call*

Jimmy Yancey, *How Long Blues*

Otis Spann, *Spann's Boogie*

Little Brother Montgomery, *Bass Key Boogie*

OTHER BARRELHOUSE BASSES

Barrelhouse Buck, *Mercy Blues*

Jesse James, *Lonesome Day Blues*

Appendix B—Record Company Addresses

Archive of Folk Music
c/o Everest Enterprises Inc.
10920 Wilshire Blvd.
West Los Angeles, CA 90024

Arhoolie Records
(also Blues Classics)
Box 9195
Berkeley, CA 94709

Atlantic Records
1841 Broadway
New York, NY 10023

Biograph Records
(also Historical)
P.O. Box 109
Canaan, NY 12029

Blues Classics: see Arhoolie

Delmark Records
4243 North Lincoln
Chicago, IL 60618

Folkways Records
(also RBF)
43 West 61st Street
New York, NY 10023

Historical: see Biograph

Milestone Records
10th & Parker Streets
Berkeley, CA 94710

Origin Jazz Library (OJL)
P.O. Box 14068
San Francisco, CA 94114

RBF: see Folkways

Storyville Records
Jydeholmen 15
DK-2720 Vanlose, Denmark

Swaggie Records
Box 125, P.O. South Yarra
Victoria, 3141. Australia

Testament Records
507 Palo Verde Avenue
Pasadena, CA 91107

Yazoo Records
54 King Street
New York, NY 10014

Alex Moore

Piano Red

Boogie Woogie Red at the 1972 Ann Arbor Blues Festival.

Meade Lux Lewis

Memphis Slim

Dave Alexander